T0199123

I will praise you because I have been
remarkably and wondrously made. Your works
are wondrous, and I know this very well.
PSALM 139:14

# Black Girls Lives Matter Too!!

VALERIE

LYNN

ABRAMS

WestBow Press books may be ordered through booksellers or by contacting:

WestBow Press
A Division of Thomas Nelson & Zondervan
1663 Liberty Drive
Bloomington, IN 47403
www.westbowpress.com
844-714-3454

ISBN: 978-1-6642-7365-8 (sc)
ISBN: 978-1-6642-7366-5 (e)

Library of Congress Control Number: 2022913683

Print information available on the last page.

WestBow Press rev. date: 08/19/2022

WestBow
PRESS®
A DIVISION OF THOMAS NELSON
& ZONDERVAN

If we say, "We have fellowship with him, and yet we walk in darkness, we are lying and are not practicing the truth. If we walk in the light as he himself is in the light, we have fellowship with one another, and the blood of Jesus his Son cleanses us from all sin."

1 John 1:6-7

Black Girls Lives Matter Too!!

# Dedication

Without my dearest parents, The Late Mr. &

Mrs. Nathaniel & Elizabeth Davis, this book

would not have made its way to the bookstores.

I'm forever grateful for their support and their

example of love and spiritual guidance. It was

an honor and privilege to care for the both of

them. Happy Hallelujah to my parents whose

in Heaven with each other, and it's more

gratifying being with Jesus Christ Lord of all!

Dear Reader,

In writing this book, I find the most awareness is that my Savior has provided us with much light and strength, even in the darkness that keeps lurking our way. I know without a doubt that my Savior has a plan for our life. No matter what it looks like I believe my Savior will never leave us nor will He forsake us. Don't get me wrong, there were times I thought my Savior was not hearing my prayers. However my faith has sustained me because I truly believe the word of God is true. I wait patiently on my Savior for His divine answer, which can be instant or years. He has prepared everything for His purpose.

He has also created abundant resources and we are taking advantage of them.

I hope you will too!

Valerie Lynn Abrams

My amazing life began with me being adopted into a two parent Christian home.

**Black Girls Lives Matter Too!!**

My mom told me bedtime stories about how she and my dad were adopted into the family of Jesus Christ.

For you did not receive a spirit of slavery to fall back into fear. Instead, you received the spirit of adoption, by whom we cry out "Abba Father!"

Romans 8:15

Black Girls Lives Matter Too!!

Those bedtime stories made it easier for me to understand how privileged I was to be adopted by my parents.

**Black Girls Lives Matter Too!!**

When I was a little girl, I knew without a doubt that I was blessed. I had friends and family of all races to love and play with me. I showed them love too.

So God created man in his own image; he created him in the image of God; he created them male and female. Genesis 1:27

**Black Girls Lives Matter Too!!**

**Black Girls Lives Matter Too!!**

I did **not** recognize the color of my friend's skin in a negative way, because my parents taught me that God created and love all people.

Trust the Lord with all your heart, and do not rely on your own understanding, in all your ways know him, and he will make your paths straight.

Proverbs 3:5-6

Black Girls Lives Matter Too!!

**Black Girls Lives Matter Too!!**

As my school days begun, my parents wanted me to be well rounded in all areas of my life. They wanted me to have the best education academically, spiritually, physically and for that they enrolled me into a said Private Christian School. There were very few Brown and Black people in attendance.

If I speak human or angelic tongues but do not have love, I am a noisy gong or a clanging cymbal.

1 Corinthians 13:1

**Black Girls Lives Matter Too!!**

**Black Girls Lives Matter Too!!**

In the beginning the boys, girls, teachers, staff, and parents showed me and my family an enormous amount of **love**.

Not paying back evil for evil or insult for insult but, on the contrary, giving a blessing, since you were called for this, so that you may inherit a blessing.

1 Peter 3:9

**Black Girls Lives Matter Too!!**

**Black Girls Lives Matter Too!!**

Something happened that caused me to feel all alone. My mom and I no longer felt loved. Initially we could not wrap our mind around it at all.

Pray constantly…

1 Thessalonians 5:17

**Black Girls Lives Matter Too!!**

**Black Girls Lives Matter Too!!**

There was a time we could not get inside the building. I became sad and my mom was terribly upset. So, she prayed, and she prayed, and she prayed for me without quitting.

I will lead the blind by a way they did not know;

I will guide them on paths they have not known.

I will turn darkness to light in front of them and

rough places into level ground. This is what I

will do for them, and I will not abandon them.

Isaiah 42:16

**Black Girls Lives Matter Too!!**

**Black Girls Lives Matter Too!!**

Hallelujah! Hallelujah! My mom decided to withdraw me from that school. She felt strongly that Jesus was leading her to do so. I praise and thank Jesus for it.

God is our refuge and strength, a helper

who is always found in times of trouble.

Psalms 46:1

**Black Girls Lives Matter Too!!**

**Black Girls Lives Matter Too!!**

There are times I no longer want to live.

Because of my parents' constant prayers and love, in addition to my faith, it has kept me alive.

For his anger lasts only a moment, but his favor, a lifetime. Weeping may stay overnight, but there is joy in the morning.

Psalms 30:5

**Black Girls Lives Matter Too!!**

There is no doubt that every

Black girl life matters.

In addition, **all** girls' lives matter, no matter

what the race is! Through it all I am so

grateful for my faith that has sustained

me and caused me to intentionally

try to follow the ways of Jesus.

*Valerie, my sister, cousin, and my friend, is a giving and* **kind-hearted person.** *She is an aggressively enterprising person and an achiever in everything she does. Congrats and much success in this new endeavor as an author. Love you!*

BRENDA REID, FOREVER FAMILY

*Valerie is a phenomenal person whom I find to be very* **Intelligent and Thought Provoking.** *She is a very energetic confident person who always makes you feel loved.*

LISA MORRIS, FRIEND FOR MANY YEARS

*Valerie is a one-of-a-kind person. When I say this, I truly mean an extraordinary individual with a* **"Great Big Heart."** *She loves straight from her heart, and you know it because you can feel it. I know that God rewards her because of her* **Faith and Believeth in Christ.** *She is very genuine and loving. I appreciate her for never changing and always being that friend/sister to whom you can depend. Congratulations friend for all your hard work.*

VICKI JACKSON, FRIEND FOR OVER 40 YEARS

*Valerie has always* **pursued excellence** *in everything she does. This new "chapter" in her life will be no exception. Congratulations!!!*

NORMAN & LAVONNE JOHNSON, GODPARENTS OF THE ABRAMS' DAUGHTER

*This is such an honor! When I met Valerie Lynn, she was Green, not Abrams. We have been friends and* **prayer confidants** *for an exceptionally long time. If she tells you that she is going to do something, you can believe that it will be done. This book is such an accomplishment, I am not surprised. She is* **amazing and an ambitious person!** *What a wonderful book. I am looking for more to come! Congratulations my friend.*

PAT M. SLATER, FRIEND FOR OVER 40 YEARS

Printed in the United States
by Baker & Taylor Publisher Services